Paperback ISBN: 979-8-9904849-6-2
eBook ISBN: 979-8-9904849-7-9
Hardcover: 979-8-9904849-6-6

LYME LLC
www.lyme4u.com
INFO@lyme4u.com

Dedication

This book is dedicated to my two beautiful daughters Marian and Riyan, my loving mother Edith, my darling sister Carla, and my supportive family and friends. A very special thanks to Mr. and Mrs. Abraham and Barbara Jean Gainer, my other parents, for your great advice and insightful conversations about everything from growing a garden to politics. Thanks to my niece London and nephew Davion Booth for their humorous feedback. You all inspire me in a very special way through your love, laughter, and prayers. By God's grace, the best is yet to come!

I also dedicate this book, and others in the series, to every individual who lived through the COVID-19 pandemic. I pray our stories will fill your hearts and minds with fonder memories and better days. God Bless you!

Riyan's Backyard Adventures

"A Visitor in Our Garden"

Hi, my name is Riyan! My family and I did some fun things during a break from school and work. Schools and stores were shut down to keep everyone safe from a bad germ. I missed my teachers and friends. My mom kept us busy with fun things to do. We grew a garden on our patio. It was exciting! But there was a big surprise too!

TIMBER PARK
ELEMENTARY

SCHOOL IS CLOSED.
WE WILL MISS YOU!
STAY CONNECTED!

My big sister Marian and I were happy Mom decided to grow the plants in the screened-in patio. The screen helped keep bugs and pests out.

Mom learned about planting a garden from her grandmother. She started our gardening project with plants that were easy to grow.

To prepare for growing our garden, we first needed to buy supplies. We went to Lukas Nursery.

There was so much there to take in and see. The daisies, roses, tulips, and sunflowers were so beautiful! It was like walking through a maze of brilliant colors and shapes!

Oh, and there was a sweet fruit smell from strawberries on the vine. It was like a wonderland at the nursery!

The street signs on each corner guided us as we walked the paths. Sometimes, we would be surprised by a statue of animals and people. Mom almost jumped out of her skin when we turned to see a strange creature!

VIBURNUM CIR.

MAIN ST.

Azaleas

One of the best attractions was the Butterfly Exhibit. Some of the caterpillars had turned into beautiful butterflies. It was amazing!

We loaded our cart with flowerpots, containers, buckets, seeds, plants, potting soil, and a watering can. We also got gardening gloves and tools. I was excited to get back home to start our garden!

We filled flowerpots with soil. We also used dried seeds we saved from vegetables from the grocery store. We had bell pepper, watermelon, cucumber, and lemon seeds.

We learned there are four steps to planting seeds.

First, Marian and I used one of our fingers to make holes in the soil.

Second, we dropped a few tomato seeds in each hole.

Third, we covered the seeds with soil and watered them.

Fourth, we wrote the name of the type of fruit or vegetable on Popsicle sticks. We repeated the same steps for planting cucumbers, watermelons, and lemons until we were done. To plant the bell pepper seeds, we used a rectangular container. We had seeds for red, green, yellow, and orange bell peppers. We made rows in the dirt for each color.

I was most excited about seeing the bell peppers grow. I looked forward to eating them. Stuffed bell peppers are a favorite family meal.

The pots and containers were all placed where they could get direct sunlight. Every day my sister and I would look out onto the patio. We wanted to see if any of the seeds started growing. Mom reminded us it would take days for the seeds to sprout out of the soil.

Every other day we watered the plants.

Days later, we saw something green about to sprout.

The next day, it was like magic! There were rows of baby bell pepper plants filling the container. They were lined up like an army of soldiers standing at attention. This reminded me of Dad's time in the military.

The tomatoes and cucumbers were growing too. Each plant grew flower buds. Over time, the flowers turned into tiny fruits or vegetables. I was amazed and could hardly wait to see what would happen next!

I was surprised by what happened next! As I checked on the plants, I saw something small zip out of sight on the patio. I had to take a closer look.

It was a lizard! I could not believe it was inside the patio! The screened-in patio was supposed to be lizard and bug-free!

Before the garden, that is where my sister Marian and I would sit and watch the squirrels and rabbits play in the backyard. That is a whole other story. Anyway, I yelled for Marian to come see the visitor on our patio.

BELL PEPPERS   BELL PEPPERS

Marian and I stood at the glass patio door to watch the little creature. I noticed it looked different than the other lizards we had seen in our yard. It had a red stripe down its back. I named him Stripe for that reason. Marian agreed it was the perfect name! I liked watching Stripe having fun leaping around and sunbathing on our patio.

Stripe always seemed to freeze when he saw us. I guess he thought that would make him invisible. The only thing he moved was his eyeballs. They followed our every move. My sister and I tricked Stripe when we moved in different directions. He didn't know who to follow with his eyes. It was funny!

The next day when I looked on the patio, I was shocked to see the leaves on the bell pepper plants had been nibbled on. But none of the other plants had been touched.

"Who or what could have done this?" I asked. Stripe was still inside the patio. Mom thought it was Stripe eating the bell peppers. She was not happy about it!

My big sister said, "It can't be the lizard eating the bell pepper leaves. They eat bugs. Ewww!"

I replied, "Mom, I agree with Marian. It could not have been Stripe!"

Before I could say another word, Mom grabbed the broom! Stripe must have known what was going to happen next. As soon as he saw my mom coming onto the patio with the broom, he ran and hid. My sister and I were laughing so hard as our mom chased Stripe. He kept finding places to hide, but Mom found him every time. She finally chased him out of the patio.

The next morning, Mom was the first to check on the plants.

I heard her shout, "He's back and he is not welcomed!"
I ran to the patio door to see what was going on.

Every bell pepper leaf had been eaten! This time Stripe was
caught relaxing in the bell pepper container. His belly looked
to be full.

"Oh no, Stripe is in trouble," I sighed. I was starting to like him. This was not good.

My sister laughed and said, "Who knew? Lizards have to eat their vegetables too."

I chuckled. Then, I turned to see my Mom's facial expression. She was not smiling and was reaching for the broom.

BELL PEPPERS

BELL PEPPERS

Like an action hero, Stripe leaped off the patio table and did a free fall to the floor.

With a broom in hand, Mom rushed after him as he searched for a way out. Mom swatted at him with the broom. Stripe was ducking and dodging as best he could. He ran to the left. He ran to the right. Stripe made a mad dash outside out of sight.

The next morning, I looked onto the patio to find half of the bell pepper stems had been eaten down to the dirt.

"Mom, you are not going to believe this!" I yelled.

She and Marian came rushing onto the patio. Mom spotted Stripe on the patio table eating the bell pepper plants. He looked up to see all eyes on him.

Mom had the broom in hand once again. Stripe did not have time to freeze! He just started running for cover. I felt bad for Stripe because I knew he was in big trouble. Stripe was giving Mom a run for it. He zipped from place to place on the patio. Stripe found a lot of places to hide. Mom could not find him for a while, but she was not giving up.

Striped messed up! He made a noise that got Mom's attention. She moved a container and there was Stripe! She had him cornered. He froze. Mom told my big sister to come and hold the screen door open. Stripe made a mad dash out of the patio!

Mom was right on his tail with the broom. Poor Stripe! Mom swatted him with the broom. He stopped running. He was down!

My sister shouted, "Oh no! Stripe is not moving!"

I ran towards Stripe to see what was going on. Mom looked shocked!

"Mom, you hit him too hard. Is he still alive?" Marian asked. I looked down and Stripe was belly up!

Mom replied, "Oh my, I did not think I hit him that hard. I just wanted to give him a little nudge with the broom."

We waited to see if he would recover. Just when I started to lose hope Stripe quickly flipped over and began running towards the hedges. He darted across the brick pavers like a toy race car going full speed. Stripe had us all fooled. I didn't care. I was happy he was okay.

The joy at Stripe's recovery turned to gloom. I didn't want him to be gone forever. He may be too scared to come back. Suddenly, the sky got dark and then it started raining. We went inside our house. Mom went to her room. I walked in behind her. She was looking out her window into the backyard.

I whispered, "Do you think the clouds turned grey and the rain came because Stripe is sad? Do you think he may be gone forever?"

I reminded Mom that some of the bigger lizards can be mean. They would sometimes fight and bite each other's tails. Our patio was like a safe space for little Stripe. He was now all alone out in the open.

My sister tried to make me feel better by saying, "Maybe Stripe will make his way over to DUDA Farm to live in the big white barn. He'll probably make a lot of friends there."

Mom called for a group hug. Then, the rain stopped and the sun came back out. A beautiful rainbow appeared. It felt like God was giving us the best group hug ever!

I smiled at my Mom and said, "Stripe forgives you, Mom."

Mom jokingly replied, "I forgive Stripe too for eating my bell pepper plants!"

We all laughed.

The next morning, I saw another lizard had gotten on the patio. It had a familiar red stripe down its back.

"It can't be! Quick, come look! It's Stripe and he's back!" I shouted. I couldn't believe what I was seeing!

Marian said, "Oh no, he ate the rest of the bell pepper stems!"

Mom said, "It really is the Stripe. I cannot believe he is back!"

Stripe and Mom looked at each other. My sister and I were not sure what was going to happen next. Wow! Mom did not reach for a broom.

We were all so happy Stripe returned. We no longer cared that he ate all the bell pepper plants. Marian and I planted more and kept them on a small table in the kitchen instead.

Whenever we decided to go out on the patio, Stripe would keep his distance by hanging on the window screen. He became a welcomed visitor after all.

EAT YOUR VEGETABLES!

THE END

This Book Belongs To:

About The Author:

GLORIA T. WILLIAMS is the Owner of LYME LLC. Her mission is to provide products that will inspire and comfort you! LYME stands for "Let Your Mind Elevate". Gloria obtained her Bachelor's degree in Business Management from Savannah State University; and later a Master's in Business Administration from Webster University. She is a woman of faith who believes, "With God, all things are possible." Gloria has always had a passion for storytelling and writing. With the inspiration of her two beautiful daughters, Marian and Riyan, she began her journey in writing a captivating children's book series centered on true life events. To learn more about her other books, please scan the QR Code, or visit www.lyme4u.com:

If you love this book, please take a moment to leave an Amazon review. To learn more about LYME LLC products, please visit our website by scanning the QR Code. Please leave your contact information so we can keep you informed of new product releases and events.

About the Artist:

Stacy Hummel has been an artist for as long as she can remember. Her love for art started at a young age when she began writing her own adventure stories. Her work includes children's books, comics, board games, and apps. Stacy loves to listen to music when she draws, especially Rock and Alternative music. She lives near Rochester, New York with her husband and two sons. When Stacy is not working, she enjoys playing video games, traveling, and camping with her family.

Acknowledgements

To my illustrator and artist, Mrs. Stacy Hummel: Your talent, patience, and kindness have been invaluable. You brought my vision to life page-by-page with your beautiful illustrations. I am forever grateful for your dedication and creativity. I wish you and your family the best in life!

In loving memory of my late grandparents, Mr. and Mrs. Henry and Hannah Copps, and my many beloved cousins of the Hill and Rudolph ancestry: their dedication to working the land of our Lucas ancestors to provide organically grown fruits and vegetables for the family is a legacy I cherish deeply. I honor them for being the roots of my appreciation for gardening and family.

A special recognition to Mrs. Dawn Charles: Your fabulousness in growing organic vegetables and proudly displaying your harvest has been a beacon of inspiration. You are not only beautiful but incredibly handy. I was amazed to learn you built your own greenhouse and a treehouse for your grandchildren. Your efforts encourage others to pursue their own gardening dreams.

To "Black Girls Grow Gardens Nationwide": Thank you for creating a forum where information and photos can be shared, inspiring black girls like me to plant seeds for the nourishment of both body and soul. Your community has been a source of encouragement and empowerment, especially during the COVID-19 pandemic and beyond.

To Mr. Frank Bailey, Executive Director, of Grow Orlando Inc. for promoting a micro-farm network that aims to end food disparity in under-resourced communities with low wealth.

A special thanks to Ms. Carol Smith, a faithful worker at the Lowes Garden Center in Oviedo, Florida, for her outstanding customer service! She was always so helpful and kind.

Thank you all for your contributions to this book!

Made in the USA
Columbia, SC
28 November 2024